The
LONDON
CAT

By James
Dowsing

SUNRISE PRESS

34 CHURTON ST, LONDON

SCENE STEALING

OVER THE centuries London has produced more than its fair share of talented, not to say brilliant, actors. Less well known is its long line of stage-struck felines.

The Globe Theatre in Shaftesbury Avenue even had a publicity still of its most notable house cat hanging in its foyer. This was Beerbohm, named after the great actor-manager. The tabby regularly made unscheduled cameo appearances in plays, stealing scene after scene and provoking ill-feeling among the actors.

Then there was the time the stage was filled with tons of sand and flagstones for the House of Bernard Alba. To everyone's embarrassment Beerbohm mistook it for a massive litter. Also best forgotten is the night he ate the feathers in Beryl Reid's hat, and the time he attacked the collection of stuffed birds decorating a set.

Miss Reid, a noted cat enthusiast, used to take home the theatre cat at the Lyric Theatre each evening after performances. It helped to relieve the loneliness of Fleur's caretaking life; besides, as the actress noted, "All cats need looking at."

The Everyman cinema in Hampstead had five cats on its premises at one time and they loved to loll upon the projection equipment. According to one report, however, they were barred from the auditorium, apart from the matinees, when one of them leapt into a woman's lap during a frightening scene in Psycho.

ISBN 1 873876 459

One million pairs of mystic eyes ... one million noses sizing up your personality ... one million tails waving at their owners' return at the end of the day ...

Few, if any, cities have more cats than London. Add the suburban wild cats and the strays and the tally goes over 1½ million, and rising. Increasingly the English love their felines, and among urban dwellers there is special regard for a pet which seems to know how to look after itself.

Is there a London type? An exotic Asian breed may look out from a half-frosted window, or there may be a Burmese in the better-type pet shop. But for many, the London cat is that black and white individual, with a far-from-spotless bib, of stocky build, at once hard-boiled and sentimental, stand-offish yet loyal.

Its ancestors sailed in with the Romans, if not earlier, and have seen the centuries unfold. Its grandfather's grandfather knew Dick Whittington, you see, and an actual uncle kept Churchill's feet warm, though he was ginger coloured. All in all he is content with his city, knows every inch of his three-mile territory of bricks, hubbub and pagentry, and, of course, is glad within himself.

Down the Tube

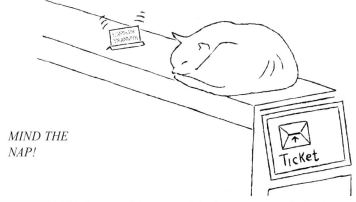

MIND THE NAP!

THE LONDON Underground has one of the longest networks in the world and yet for all its problems can surprise the traveller with a homely touch. There are the pigeons which hop aboard the Circle Line and journey to the next station; the buskers sporting animal masks – and Pebbles the tom cat who regularly snoozed on top of a ticket gate machine.

Pebbles adopted staff at the Barbican station, making himself at home in the booking hall, seemingly unfazed by the clatter of trains below and the scramble of customers. Then, for a reason known only to the feline mind, he selected a favourite automatic gate – it had to be an IN machine – and then each day at an appointed hour hopped aboard, curled up and napped the afternoon away. Never mind that those tickets popped out of the slot near his ears, and that unknown hands grabbed for the piece of card, as the gates crashed open.

Perhaps the attraction came from this constant repetition – the hiss of the ticket and the swing of the gates. Or was it the tantalising nearness of all those fingers, and their varied scents? Consider, too, how one's own cat loves to snooze when visitors call, as if to say, "These people bore me, but let them admire me if they want." The fact that Pebbles' visitors totalled many hundreds an hour is immaterial: the principle is the same.

Station staff hinted that Pebbles had introduced a friend into the Tube fold, though this feline kept out of the limelight. Certainly rodents were no problem about the place, and what was to stop Pebbles and escort from venturing into those interesting tunnels after midnight when the Metropolitan, Circle and Hammersmith lines closed down? No road traffic to worry about, just miles and miles of silent, twisting track to be explored. No wonder Pebbles purred upon his automated perch.

The Savoy jinx

ONCE A MONTH a very singular club meets at this premier London hotel where its proceedings are watched over by the all-knowing gaze of a black feline mascot called Caspar. Members include leading politicans, service chiefs and creative luminaries.

The Other Club began in its present form through the efforts in 1911 of a rising politican by name of Winston Churchill, aided by the future Lord Birkenhead. Upon a shelf, before a gleaming mirror, rests Caspar, who knows every secret, has seen the fortunes of the initiated rise and fall, and plays a central role in a particular taboo. This states that no member must be allocated the thirteenth place when members sit down at table in the Pinafore Room.

In this same hotel, on the Strand, at the turn of the century fourteen associates were booked to meet; one cancelled, and the thirteenth diner, one Joel Woolf, a mining magnate, was subsequently shot dead in his office in South Africa.

So today, to avoid tempting fate, Caspar fills the No. 13 place and is provided with napkin, cutlery and wine glass. He has taken this role for the last seventy-odd years, and has won a place of affection in the hearts of members. Previously a member of staff had been roped in but in the 1920s the artist Basil Ionides was commissioned to create a life-like cat, and so Caspar was carved out of the wood of a plane tree. In this way the feline family was called on yet again to exercise that same magic power, for good or ill, that has fascinated man through the ages.

• Sir Richard Whittington gives his lucky cat a tickle in this later engraving of the Lord Mayor of London. With the help of his cat he rose to fame and fortune, or so legend would have it. Both are recalled today by memorials at Archway, North London, and at St. Michael Paternoster Row in the City.

Mouser honoured

TOO FEW Londoners are aware of it but an image of Dick Whittington's cat can be seen at the spot near Highgate where the young man turned to listen to the Bow Bells.

It was placed there in the 1960s, on top of an existing monument erected some 140 years earlier to mark the site, on the west side of Highgate Hill facing north. (Tube: Archway on Northern Line, High Barnet branch. Highgate Hill begins outside station.)

The stone carving of the cat shows it in a squatting position, with head turned as if also responding to the bells. Both the feline image and the original monument were put in place through the initiative of public-spirited citizens.

The site is reached just before the corner with Magdala Avenue and the **Whittington Hospital**. The diminutive monument, within its oval shaped railing, was placed on the pavement near the edge of the road and can so easily be missed.

Nearby is the **Whittington Stone** pub and further up the hill the **Whittington and Cat**, which contains in a back room the skeleton of a cat, held in a wooden frame on the wall. This, the barman said, was the authentic remnant of Dick's pet. Some regular patrons nodded sagely. Until 1970 almshouses were situated in the vicinity, having been endowed by Dick in his later years.

• Another image of the famed, no-name cat can be admired in stained glass at

St. Michael Paternoster Royal, College St., beside Cannon St. Station.

Here it is almost a tabby and its tail rises into the air, while Dick in his flat cap has a tough determined look. Above them shine the towers of London, city of gold.

The window is the work of John Hayward and the style reflects the 1960s when the church was restored after wartime bombing. It is now the headquarters of the Missions to Seamen.

The delightful Wren building stands on the site of an earlier church paid for by Whittington. He was buried here on the south side of the altar beside his wife, but all trace was lost in the Great Fire. Next to the church, in **College Hill**, a plaque, at No. 19–20, recalls that Dick's house stood on this site. The reference to a college stems from an institution which he had financed.

Today College Hill and vicinity contain much charm, the street slopping narrowly down to what then would have been the Thames waterfront. Some guild houses, such as those of the skinners and dyers, stand nearby, amid a jumble of smaller offices and courts.

St. Mary-le-Bow, of the renowned chimes, still rises grandly above Cheapside, though the church which Dick knew was a victim of the Great Fire, to be re-built by Wren. On the other side of the street, at the corner with Ironmonger Lane, can be seen the hall of the **Mercer's Company**, of which Whittington was a leading light. The present building dates only from the 1950s.

•   •   •

For some years the City of London's own museum, at the Barbican, helped to keep Dick's memory alive by using as its logo a sketch of the young Richard and his cat striding off the meet their destiny.

According to the tale, Dick was an orphan, reduced to sleeping in doorways. One

• The logo of the Museum of London which depicted Dick Whittington and his cat heading off on their travels. In later years Dick rose to be a leading City dignatory and benefactor to many causes and institutions, as well as holding the office of mayor.

TOP OF
THE BILL

CATS, the musical, lifted the feline family into a new, glittering realm. Every cat-lover knew they were stars, and every cat instinctively agreed, but at the New London Theatre Andrew Lloyd Webber made their wiles, egos and mating habits the centre of an entire West End show.

Some of the theatre pros shook their heads. "An evening about cats – barmy!" However, the producers had as their base that collection of verse of the inter-war years, Old Possum's Book of Practical Cats, written by T. S. Eliot and influenced by Edward Lear.

Though Lloyd Webber had his odd stage disappointment up to that time Cats was not to be one of the flops. From 1981 weekly grosses have ticked over pleasantly year on year in London and around the world.

Eliot, who was American born, taught briefly at Highgate School in North London after studies at Oxford. Then followed eight years in the service of Lloyds Bank which almost brought him to a nervous collapse since he was also moonlighting, cat like, on literary projects. By the time the Possum collection was published, however, in 1939, he was established as a leading creative figure in the English-speaking world and beyond.

• Like any feline enterprise, the opening night of Cats in May, 1981 came with a dash of ill luck, or black magic, call it what you will. A bomb threat was received during the performance, sending cast and audience into the street. But a hit show rises above all obstacles, and amid much good humour the performers received a massive ovation at the end – a legend was born.

For Lloyd Webber the show had been more than the usual showbiz gamble. He had branched out minus Tim Rice, though now he had director Trevor Nunn to marshal the considerable resources on hand. Not least was the theatre's revolving stage to which were added seating for the audience, since the theatregoer was to be involved as much as possible; cat models were placed throughout the theatre, along with piles of rubbish to make any feline lick its chops. In fact, the garbage was enlarged three-and-a-half times to put it into cat's scale, while scattered about the stage and auditorium were 600 pairs of cat's eyes – enthralling, seemingly alive.

Audiences loved John Napier's designs and enjoyed such tricks as Rumpus being catapulted through the trap door and Mr. Mistoffolee's jacket covered in 370 tiny lights. By 1996 Cats had broken the West End and Broadway records for longest-running musical and at its sixteenth birthday had been seen by seven million people in Drury Lane alone.

evening he picked as his resting place the steps of a merchant, one Fitzwarren, who spotted the urchin and brought him inside. He was given the job of cook's helper, and an attic, which was not only cold but infested with vermin. Enter, the mouser, bought for a song, and at least one problem was solved.

Soon Dick grows weary of scouring pans and with his wordly goods strung from a pole sets off to see the world. He had reached the outskirts of north London when fate again stepped in.

Turn again Whittington, Lord Mayor of London
Turn again Whittington, thrice Mayor of London

The Bow Bells had spoken and Dick and puss went back to the merchant's house. The chronological order of the story can vary but somehow the cat, and its mousing ability, help to make the young man's fortune in a distant land. The country had been over-run with mice until the cat set to work; elated, the ruler rewards his efforts with samples from his immense treasure trove. Dick has the capital he needs, marries Fitzwilliam's daughter and sets up as a mercer.

He prospered and in time supplied luxury fabrics to the royal court and lent large sums to Henry IV and Henry V – all in all, he became one of the most influential men of the City, and clearly, was a masterly spinner of a good tale as well.

Miaow, Minister

IN THE MIDST of World War II, as fire-bombs fell upon London, Winston Churchill found solace through the presence of a tom cat named Jack who in the age-old way would curl up at the PM's feet while he slept.

Fifty years later one of Churchill's successors, John Major, found that another tom cat could bring some domestic normality to his life while political troubles swirled around Downing Street. Humphrey, a black and white feline, became a national figure as a result of his typical tom wanderings and alleged scrapes with ducklings in St. James's Park.

The adventurer often posed for the cameras, with a wild-eyed gaze, while resting on the pavement before No. 10. Then the six-year-old went missing for an extended period in the middle of one of Mr. Major's worst periods. Could this desertion be the last straw for the PM? the Press asked.

The days went by; there were unconfirmed sightings at St. James's Park tube station and at other places throughout the West End. Someone telephoned to say he had been seen in Scotland. Staff at No. 10 wondered whether media attention had become too much for his evasive feline nature.

Had they been too quick to accuse Humphrey over the baby robins – favourites of the Prime Minister – which had been found dead in the back garden? Should they

• Mrs. Blair lets Humphrey know he can stay on at No. 10, despite gossip to the contrary.

ROAD HUMPHS!

HUMPHREY the Downing Street cat has narrowly avoided becoming the Downing Street SPLAT!

An alert No.10 aide pulled the puss from the path of Bill Clinton's two-ton bullet-proof Cadillac as the President left after his talks with Tony Blair.

An insider said: "He'd have been flattened. It was the closest we came to a diplomatic incident."

Our View: Page Eight

CLINTON: Two-ton car

NEW LABOUR: NEW DUCK SLAUGHTERED

KILLER: No 10's Humphrey

HUMPHREY the No 10 cat was in the doghouse last night after eating a Queen's duckling.

The Downing Street moggie nabbed the baby mallard from St James's Park in front of Buckingham Palace, one of his favourite hunting grounds.

The killing came just hours after Cherie Blair, wife of Premier Tony, hugged Humphrey to end rumours she wanted him evicted because she hates cats.

A witness to the duck's death said: "I saw Humphrey in Downing Street with this fluffy duckling in his mouth.

"He looked like the cat that got the cream."

Humphrey is already suspected over four missing robin nestlings at No 10 and many mouse murders. Premier Blair

By ALEX COHEN

may apologise to Her Majesty for the latest slaughter when he pops round for an audience at the Palace.

A Downing Street spokesman said "Humphrey will be up before Cabinet Secretary Sir **Robin** Butler to explain himself in the morning."

• Malicious Press reports often accused Humphrey of assaults on wildlife in the vicinity.

really have put him on strict rations after the delicacies of the official table had begun to upset his kidneys?

When hope had gone, suddenly one bright morning the rover returned, ambling down Downing Street and casting a scornful eye at the police guards, as if he had never been away. It was all such typical feline behaviour and it seemed to strike cords with the electorate.

Later it was learned that Humphrey had spent his time in the vicinity of the Tate Gallery, just half a mile away. He was drawn not by the art works but more by the nearby buildings of the Royal Army Medical Corps. whose kitchen could well have been the attraction.

• **Churchill's cat Jack**, of a marmalade shade, was fortunate in being based at Chartwell, the PM's country house in Kent. When the cat's war service was done he was laid to rest in the pet's cemetery on the estate, which consisted chiefly of dog internments. However, to perpetuate his memory Chartwell has aimed to have a ginger cat on the premises ever since.

Crimea Tom

AMONG THE weapons and artworks at the **National Army Museum**, Chelsea, in a quiet corner on the first floor, there squats one of the too-often-missed stars: Crimea Tom, survivor of the siege of Sebastapol.

Nearly 150 years have passed since then but his eyes are as bright as ever, his coat perfection in shades of brown, dappled on the body, stripped on tail and legs. A narrow collar tugs at his neck.

When Russia's leading naval base in the Black Sea fell on September 9th, 1855, the British and French forces found death and confusion everywhere. But amid the rubble was Tom, a little thin on it but clearly a born winner.

Captain William Gair, of the 16th Dragoon Guards, took charge and carefully fed and groomed him back to his old self. Tom was particularly lucky since Captain Gair held a high post in the commissary, which the cat soon discovered looked after the army's food supplies.

Not surprisingly Tom appears well rounded and content in a contemporary painting, which shows three officers, including Captain Gair, in their make-shift quarters at Sebastapol. The work, by **John Luard**, hangs near the cat's real self at the museum.

In the painting Tom rests on a box, placed centrally, and quietly ponders life's ups and downs. The artist, aged just 17 at the time, shows the cat in dark shades, almost black, with white chest.

Luard was the brother of Captain Richard Luard, who is thought to be the central

The Welcome Arrival by John Luard, with Crimea Tom resting on table, centre.

figure in the piece. The men are unpacking boxes from home, hence the title, A Welcome Arrival.

The artist was visiting his brother at Sebastapol soon after the lifting of the siege. The work was completed in 1857, three years before the painter's death, and was presented to the museum by a Luard descendant.

(Museum, in Royal Hospital Road, open 10–5.30 every day. Free. Tube: Sloane Square, then walk up the King's Road. Turn left at Smith St. or similar, then further short step south to museum.)

• *GINGER DOWN BELOW*

The Blackwall road tunnel in the East End proved to have a compelling fascination for one ginger cat. After being found by workmen, as a kitten, hiding behind a fire hydrant in the tunnel he opted to stay on as a kind of mascot. He made his home in the maintenance area and appeared oblivious to the fumes and noise of the traffic. Best of all he enjoyed the weekly hoovering which staff gave him to remove the grit and grime from his coat.

The owl and the pussy cat

THE CREATOR of the well-loved poem, Edward Lear, was born and raised in North London, at Holloway, which in the early years of the 19th century could attract aspiring City types. Lear senior began as a fruiterer and sugar refiner, as had other members of his family; later he turned to dabbling in shares. The house, Bowman's Lodge, stood on the corner of Seven Sisters and Holloway Roads – now a nightmarish traffic intersection – but in Lear's time part of outer London. Today, only the name of a tiny street, Bowman's Place survives.

Edward was the youngest of a brood of 21, and while very young his father's stock dealings brought the Lears to near ruin. The family broke up and Edward, who was never robust, was reared by his eldest sister. These circumstances, one feels, set the course of his life. He shied from matrimony and wandered the world, dogged periodically by melancholia, until well into his later years. Indeed, The Owl and the Pussy Cat appeared in a new volume of nonsense songs in 1871, the year he at last made his final home, at San Remo. Here he took up residence with his own feline, Foss.

• *Edward Lear... Never constitutionally strong he earned a living from the age of 15 as an artist, specialising in natural history. The British Museum and Zoological Society were among his earliest employers. Later the wide world called.*

Lear began to earn a living from his drawings at the age of 15 when his output showed an increasing emphasis on natural history. He worked for the Zoological Society, which still runs London Zoo, and later the British Museum. As a diversion he wrote nonsense poems for the amusement of the grandchildren of his patron, the Earl of Derby, and the first collection of these works was published in 1846. Meanwhile, he turned to landscape painting on his tours of Egypt, Syria and further afield. These wonderfully evocative works can be seen at the British Museum and the Tate, though many of the watercolours only appear for special exhibitions.

• Lear's illustration for
his own poem

GHOSTLY ONE

London's oldest brewery, Fuller's, beside the Thames, claims to be haunted by the miaowing of the unlucky cat which went too near the edge of a sugar dissolving vessel in the 1950s. Confident of its footing, like all felines, and curious to a fault, it tumbled into the boiling mixture and perished before staff could come to the rescue.

Fuller's Griffin Brewery at Chiswick is open to the public for tours on Monday, Wednesday, Thursday, Friday at 11am, noon, 1pm and 2pm. Sightings of the spectral cat, however, cannot be guaranteed. The establishment is small in scale and guides like to point out what is believed to be the oldest wisteria plant in the country growing healthily upon the brickwork. Nearby is the home of the painter Hogarth, which is also open to view, while a stroll down Chiswick Mall on the Thames front gives hints of Whistler and any number of riverscape specialists.

Near-relatives of our family cat

THE BIG CATS are well represented in the Regent's Park enclosures and have included, for example, the endangered Sumatran Tiger. But the zoo has also contained interesting members of the smaller brigade which bear even more striking similarities with the domestic pet.

There has been the Sand Cat *(Felis margarita)*, which ranges through the semi-desert area of northern Africa, Arabia and south-western Asia. Mainly yellow to brown and equipped with large ears to aid night-time hunting it has been suspected of reaching the at-risk category, or worse.

An even more intriguing occupant of the zoo has been the Clouded Leopard, a shy, nocturnal creature from the forests of South-East Asia. Beautifully marked with marbled blotches, spots and stripes it is vulnerable to man's attentions; in behaviour and design it seems to fall somewhere between the big and small cats.

Our household tabby *(Felis catus)* – sitting on a soft cushion in countless homes encircling Regent's Park – is, of course, also an accredited member of the felis (small cat) family, and the external likeness with its often secretive, seldom-seen relatives of the Andes cannot be ignored. The London cat, however, stalking through the tomato

• *The Kaffir Cat, often thought to be the forefather of the household cat. Found in Syria, Egypt and parts of Africa it is smaller than the European Wild Cat, and is coloured yellowish buff to grey, with horizontal bands.*

plants of a back garden, possibly came here with the Romans, if not sooner, and owes its domestication to the ancient Egyptians, who adopted the African wildcat or marsh and jungle variants.

So it is not without cause that our pets hold their heads high and regard us from time to time with a disdainful air. After all their family tree ranges from the short-tail lynx to the tiny (4lb.) flat-headed cat of southern Asia, the ocelot of the New World, with its prized coat, and the pampas cat of South America. But what of the relative which looks more like a weasel, the laguarondi, of the same region, which sports small ears, a snub nose and short legs? Actually, "We don't talk about them."

BEYOND THE PALE

London wildcats are out there, in the shadows – no doubt about it – but estimating their number can be as hazardous as the life they lead. A scholar at the University of Bradford, P. Rees, made a study in the 1980s and found that the UK population of ferals was about one million. London was thought to be over represented since kind-hearted Londonders helped promote their spread with their generous handouts, supplementing the usual diet of rodents, other mammals, birds, reptiles and insects.

Within the factory sites and abandoned buildings of the capital live large numbers of cats who through ill-luck or preference fight it out with man and nature. They can be divided between those born to this state and those who – more disturbing to cat lovers – have run away from comfortable homes.

Though brilliantly designed as hunters the ferals obtain most of their food through scavenging and charity feeding, a sad state for a creature so rightly proud. They like the company of their fellows, which leads to the setting up of colonies in London and other urban areas. Within these, however, there is scope for small groups who hive off for resting, not to mention the usual loners.

For the pampered feline of Islington or Cheam, brushing the legs of his or her protector, the ferals lurking at the end of the alleyway are a temptation and a fascination. Some pets weaken and fall, as every cat owner well knows.

Egypt on the T1

AMID ALL the great treasures of the British Museum special prominence has been given, rightly, to a stunning effigy of an Egyptian cat – the Gayer-Anderson – which shines in its green coat of bronze adorned with nose and ear-rings and necklet.

It is one of a series of exhibits which highlight the religious and magical significance of our domestic cat through the ages. Its wild and big cat relatives are featured, too, but it is the small household pet as we know it that commands much attention.

In a museum which is so strong on Egyptian finds this is fitting since our tabby may well have come from North Africa via the camp fires and temples of the Nile civilisation.

And, unknown to most visitors, this same institution contains its own in-house collection of living, breathing felines who emerge each day as the last tourists head for their hotels . . .

*   *   *

The Gayer-Anderson Cat, named after one of its donors, sits upright in the Egyptian galleries, coolly eyeing the parade of visitors.

It is from the Roman era, after 30 BC, yet behind its sleek exterior the sculpture exhibits all the strangeness and mystery of the earliest times, for here is an embodiment of the goddess Bastet.

The museum possesses further tributes to the feline world: cases full of mummified cats and kittens from Abydos, Thebes and elsewhere, and a representation of the Cat of Re dissecting the serpent Apophis in the Book of the Dead papyrus of about 1310 BC.

This image demonstrates the importance of the cat in pest control during ancient times and fits well with a similar role played by a team of moggies within the museum today. At dusk, or sooner, these unpaid heroes and heroines leave their little carpeted lairs and begin a tour of duty.

No doubt it is impossible, but one can visualise such slightly jaded veterans of the London streets ambling by the Gayer-Anderson cat at midnight sniffing and miaowing a greeting.

This group of tabbies and London black and whites has been in the care of an aged guardian, who revealed that pigeons added variety to his charges' diet and the tally could number in the thousands.

A lucky tourist may see a moggie on occasion strolling between the front portico columns or basking in the sunshine, but it is rare. One afternoon, when the portico was almost empty, a keen-eyed black specimen with white boots and bib sat unconcerned in the middle of the porch, blocking my path. As officious as any human warder he observed me with faint disdain. When our impasse had become tedious he flicked his

mes

The mystery of the Nile civilisation radiates from the Gayer-Anderson Cat, probably the noblest, most decorated feline in London. Yet even the humblest tabby carries some of the same dignity and sense of magic. It watches and is never owned.

irregular tail and returned to the base of a column to begin his toilet. Master of the Nile . . . and the Thames.

• The museum also has two other striking images of cats from Egypt. In the first, a fragment of a mural, the artist shows a cat taking an important role in a hunting expedition. As a high official, with wife and daughter, float through the marshes their cat leaps up toward a passing bird.

It seems cats were used to disturb game lurking among the papyrus flowers so that fowlers could slay them with boomerangs; possibly they also gathered in the stunned birds.

Among the museum's collection of drawings on papyrus there is a delightful satirical sketch from the New Kingdom in which animals take the place of humans, in modern cartoon style. One panel shows a cat shepherding geese; another has two lions, one of which is playing a board game. A further damaged panel appears to depict portions of a couple of cats, and a lion.

• At the start of the Egyptian Gallery visitors are greeted by the gaping jaws – MGM style – of the Lion of Nimrod, brought from the Temple of Ishtor. The red granite head dates from the reign of Amenophis III and carries the name of Tutenhamon.

• On loan from the Queen are a pair of leopards, in miniature, which were made for the royal court of Benin, West Africa. From a distance, as they stand side by side in a glass case, they could pass for twin domestic cats, rather cuddly in their stylised design. They have been created from sections of ivory fitted together, while the spots are nothing more than percussion caps which detonated 19th century rifles.

NATURAL HISTORY MUSEUM, South Kensington. This offshoot of the BM displays in its mammals section two relatives of the London cat – though both a little on the untamed side.

Sharing a case with a jaguar, cheetah and other kin are stuffed examples of the **Scottish Wild Cat** and the **Snow Leopard**. One is struck immediately by the closeness in appearance and size with our domesticated feline.

The Scottish Wild Cat is a sub species of the wildcats which live in the low mountain forests of Western Europe. It is more heavily built than our house pet and the tail is shorter and ends bluntly, while the outline of the head is altogether broader.

The Snow Leopard roams the Himalayas and Hindu Kush and is equipped with a prolific coat to keep out the chill. It is one size up again from the wild cat, but in its museum case, beside the lion and tiger, it seems endearingly toy.

Nearby, an **American Bobcat** is seen in action in a photographic blowup as it lunges at a Snowshoe hare, stressing the point that the cat family represents the true meat eaters – the most eager members of the order carnivora.

£200,000 GRAVE

London cat-lovers were agog when a dead feline's headstone sold for £200,000 at auction in the capital. One curious Tom-cat lurking around Sotherby's in New Bond Street, Mayfair, cried out: "Blimey, I'm worth more dead and buried than alive, if only for my tombstone. On second thoughts make it a million pounds."

The auctioneers had revealed that the monument, erected on the grave of a pet moggie, was in fact a re-used carving from the 9th century AD and depicted a half-length figure of St. Peter.

Stonemason Johnny Beeston found it in a quarry and – unaware of its historic importance – thought it would make a suitable memorial for Winkle, a tabby. Mrs. Beeston agreed and the stone was put in place. One day a local historian was passing their Somerset cottage and took a closer look at the object. Its significance was apparent. Measuring 16in. by 17in. the carving probably dated from the time of King Alfred (849-899).

Following Mr Beeston's death in 2003 his widow decided to put the carving on the market, much gratified by Sotheby's estimate of £60,000. Bidding was spirited and ultimately a private collector won the day with an offer of £201,600. The London Tom, on the spot, observed: "Winkle must have been some cat. Never mind King Alfie."

Hidden in couple's garden.

London feline miscellany

ROMAN MOGGIES. The domestic cat graced the early settlements in London of the Roman invaders – and may have left paw-prints to prove it. In the Museum of London's splendid display on the Roman period observant visitors will see tiny paw marks forever set in a builder's roof tile.

Could it be a dog? A lamb perhaps, or some other creature? No one at the museum was entirely certain, but whatever the origin it gives new meaning to the term "a night on the tiles". Actually, the prints would have been impressed while the freshly-made tiles were lying in the tiler's yard waiting to dry. Many examples of such animal contrariness are preserved in archaeological backrooms.

Then there are the tiny skeletons which have been unearthed from Roman sites in the City of London. At its store in Hoxton the museum's archaeological service has any number of these possible remains of felines which roamed the alleys of Londonium or purred in the laps of Roman matrons seated in parlours just like the wonderful interior re-creations on show in the museum. The more fortunate pets of that time had a standard of life equal in many ways to our own with central heating, fancy ceramics and sophisticated colour coordinations.

The little skeletons, carefully cleaned, preserved and labelled, rest in their containers upon shelves at the Eagle Wharf Road store. Though not on view to the public they demonstrate once more that domestic animals go on and on. The tile with the paw mark at the museum can be seen affixed to the railing which surrounds the reconstruction of a grand dining room of about 300 AD. This gorgeous example of Roman decor includes on the floor the Bucklesbury mosaic unearthed in the City.

LONDON CAT SHOW has brought together some of the finest pedigree felines for public admiration over more than one hundred years, and during the 1960s its scope was widened with the addition of household pets. In its centenary year of 1996 it drew a bewildering range of sizes and types, divided for judging into Oriental, Burmese, British Shorthair and Siamese, to name just some.

Initially it was held at the Crystal Palace at Sydenham and early guiding lights included Harrison Weir, founder of the National Cat Club, and the cat artist Louis Wain. These days the event takes place in the equally atmospheric **Olympia**, whose huge domed Grand Hall could be mistaken for a Brunel railway creation. Within the complex at Kensington the cat show regularly used the smaller National Hall each

December. Following the centenary success, however, the **National Cat Club** decided to move the show to the Grand Hall in order to house the buoyant entries, and trade and breed clubs' stands.

The cat club secretary Rosemary Gowdy stressed that the event was anything but static. New breeds were being admitted, and had included such seeming exotics as the **Ocicat** and **Bengal**, both very vocal and spotted, and from America, the **Maine Coon**. The other cats pretended not to notice these parvenues, of course, but how could they fail to hear them?

In the 1990s the show added a grand finale – a National Cat of the Year award – to the events on the centre stage, and a **World of Cats** exhibition highlighting the various pedigree cats around the world. For the centenary celebrations BBC cameras were on hand, as well as the travelling Moscow Cat Museum. How the domesticated cat has soared and soared.

PRETTY AS A PICTURE. Dogs, large and small, are well represented in London art collections – cats less so. However, the National Gallery does own a good number of works in which cats figure prominently. They are portrayed by no less than Manet and Gainsborough, for example, though in the latter case the feline is only sketched in and is scarcely visible. ("You see that great artist was defeated by our beauty" – Moggy copy editor.)

Manet's Woman with a Cat depicts his wife Suzanne sitting in thoughtful mood, fingers touching side of head, while her black and white pet seems to catch her mood. **Gainsborough** found himself unable to complete his charming portrait of

It's the moment of truth at Crystal Palace in 1911 for this pussy.

his two young daughters. Affectionately locked together, they also cradle in their arms a cat, which never got beyond the dimmest blur – a perpetual ghost of a moggy.

Hogarth does much better in his fully realised The Graham Children. This gorgeous painting includes a goldfinch in its cage, and – bewitched by the bird – the household cat. The feline is cast in the traditional malevolent mould: with gleaming, greedy eyes it looks over the back of a chair at the bird as it trills its song.

The young master of the house also gazes up at the cage with boyish joy, oblivious to the menace, as does the capped baby. In this way, art historians have noted, Hogarth contrasts the warmth and contentment of the household with the real world outside, ever ready to pounce and destroy. Following old mediaeval thought the cat is a symbol of the forces of darkness. It would take the Victorian era to put paid to this prejudice.

The National has at least four other cat images, but these are far from satisfactory. Though **Barocci's** Madonna and Cat is a beautiful work, the white and ginger puss is seen only in the bottom corner, upon its hind legs and with back to the viewer. It is capitivated by a goldfinch being held aloft by the young John the Baptist.

Pintoricchio does little better with his Penelope and the Suitors, also from the 16th century, and originally a fresco for the Petrucci Palace in Siena. A small, anaemic-looking feline squats on the floor, its paw resting on a ball of wool, but there is no sense of play – or of life.

Among the Dutch paintings, **Judith Leyster** (1609–1660) gives animation to her A Boy and Girl with Cat and Eel. Though a cheery work, the merriment does not extend to the tabby kitten, which seems in doleful mood. In the Sleeping Maid and Her Mistress by **Nicholas Maes**, the cat at least has a mouthful of fowl for its trouble as the bemused mistress looks out at the viewer and indicates the sleeper.

*   *   *

The Wallace Collection, in Manchester Square, has something similar, again from the 17th century. Metsu depicts fish rather than poultry; as an old woman dozes in her chair, a puss edges a paw toward a dish containing the prize. In the **National Portrait Gallery** the comedian Max Walls looks fondly at his tabby, which is curled on a table top in a portrait by Maggi Hambling, thereby displaying the domestic side of a stage rascal.

CATTERIES. As the number of felines in London moves ever upward so does the need for welcoming hostels for cats when families take holidays or are posted abroad. Though susceptible to economic downturns catteries in the capital have enhanced their services so that the little darlings feel comfortable and secure.

Cattery owners report that most domestic cats adjust readily to their premises, even those left for extended periods. Felines tend to take it in their stride provided accommodation is half decent. They do not pine, all of which has helped to put cats ahead of Fido in the popularity stakes; today's busy, career-minded pet owner favours this feline independence.

Most cats stay for about two weeks at a time at catteries, though others have been known to register lengthy periods in their pens. "We've got one who has been with us for nine months," said the owner of Comfy Cats of Hayes, West London. The pet's master was overseas on business, but the cat had become such a fixture that it slept each night on his host's bed.

When London's economy took a dive in the early 1990s some poor cats were never reclaimed. "It was probably kinder that running out on them totally," said one operator. "We were able to find homes for all of those dumped on us."

Comfy Cats had this advice for anyone bringing their puss to its premises: Inoculate, feed them well before arrival, and bring some familiar item, such as an old jumper, to remind them of home. Once they can be persuaded to eat, all will be well, though some need to be coaxed with delicacies. In Comfy Cats' case one man deposited a feral cat without warning at the cattery, which did not relish the resulting show of untamed spirits.

Some owners break down in tears at the moment of farewell and others return home early from holiday. As for the cats, they rather enjoy the change of scene with new friends.

• The cost? For a cat it can be almost half that required to kennel a dog, which can be seen as a slur among haughtier cats.

A list of inspected catteries in the UK can be obtained from the Feline Advisory Bureau, a charity dedicated to the health of cats. It is based at Taeselbury, High St., Tisbury, SP3 6LD. (SAE please; donation welcome.)

THE CATS PROTECTION LEAGUE maintains six or more shelters in Greater London while its headquarters is based in Horsham, Surrey, within the gravitational pull of the capital.

It is a testament to the ever-growing popularity of cats as pets that the number of local groups – which form the backbone of the league – has grown to well over 200 and rising. A survey in the 1990s showed that 76,000 cats had been re-housed by the groups in one year alone, compared to 2339 in 1972.

The shelters are always under pressure, which presents a problem for elderly strays or others deemed unlikely to find homes. To overcome the problem some shelters have special facilities for these weary wanderers, many of whom are sponsored by league members.

The league has long experience in its field having been founded in the 1920s as a society devoted to promoting the interests of cats. One can almost hear the twitching of whiskers all over the country at words like these – do cats, of all creatures, require anyone to look after them? The statistics for strays, rejected and injured cats and kittens rehabilitated each year shows plainly that they do, despite their heightened egos.

In addition the CPL stresses the importance of public education and backs its conviction with talks in schools and the production of videos and books. The bi-monthly magazine, The Cat, has been published continuously since 1934.

The league is the oldest and largest charity in the UK solely concerned with the welfare of cats. It receives no government aid and relies upon the generosity and time of members, and especially the efforts of local groups, which on average contain no more than nineteen members, and who raise funds and rescue distressed felines in their area.

THE FACTS. As darkness descends, the streets of London are patrolled each evening by well over one million cats. They have woken from their afternoon slumber, stretched themselves, perhaps washed and preened, then launched out on the real business of life.

If one adds to this the number of housebound cats, and their feral cousins, the total of feline inhabitants of Greater London probably rises to well above 1,500,000.

Edouard Manet's Woman with a Cat in the National Gallery, London. A rapid portrayal of his wife and her pet companion, painted near the end of his life.

Even in 1993 the domestic cat population of the capital had reached the million mark. A survey published in that year by the Cats Protection League and Spillers Arthur's showed that 25 per cent of British families owned at least one cat. This represented an estimated domestic cat population of 7.6 million. Of that, nearly one-sixth could have been said to live in Greater London.

Nationwide some 1.3 million households had more than one cat while 21,920 homes had six feline mouths to feed. Hence, it is hardly surprising that UK owners spent more than £533 million on tinned and dried food for their charges in 1992. Of this amount it can be assumed that London cats scooped down some £85–90 million worth.

The Cats Protection League believes that commercially prepared food is preferable to most home-produced fare. It meets the dietary needs of cats and kittens, says the CPL, which also warns against giving milk in any form.

• **Running costs.** The cost of keeping a cat can be surprisingly high, according to the league. The day-to-day expenses, it estimates, could be £250 a year just for basic requirements. There are, of course, those 365 tins of pet food, but what about the 25 boxes of biscuits and 12 bags of litter, the worming tablets and flea powder? If you like to add fresh fish or occasional luxuries as a treat the annual bill can soar.

• **Motivation.** It is not advisable to let this information slip into the paws of your cat but the chief reason cited among British owners for keeping a feline was pure and simple love. This in spite of those unexplained disappearances, that cold indifference from time to time and the sharpening of claws on the back of the sofa.

In the CPL – Spillers Arthur's survey 31 per cent of owners cited admiration, infatuation, love – call it what you will – as the main motive for having a cat. Women were more ready to admit this than were men. Companionship came next, scoring 27 per cent, with habit at 12 per cent. The need for a cat as a companion was particularly important for Londoners where urban alienation and loneliness helped lift this factor six per cent over the national average.

• **Their cat's origin.** When it came to acquiring a cat most people in the UK turned to a friend or relative (42 per cent), though another 41 per cent said they had taken in a stray or a cat from a refuge.

MUSEUM CLOSES. A charming collection of feline artworks and memorabilia has ceased to be on show for the enjoyment of cat lovers in London. The Cat Museum in Harrow High Street, near the famous school, was founded by Kathleen Mann as part of her antique shop at No.49.

It was crammed with all manner of items ranging from at least 20 Louis Wain works to porcelain figurines, seaside souvenirs, paintings and historical engravings. Closure of this absorbing venue has left a sad gap in the capital's lineup of specialist museums.

A typical breezy creation by Louis Wain of his chosen field – cats in all kinds of guises – which earned him wide public recognition, until the cheeriness turned to tragedy in his personal life.

The cat's friend

THE TRAGIC STORY of Louis Wain, the London artist who devoted his life to the welfare of felines, has become too little known these days outside the cat fanciers' world.

As much as anyone he helped to popularise the keeping of cats yet their protector was to waste away his latter years as a pauper in a mental asylum. He died in Bethlehem Royal Hospital (Bedlam), Lambeth, now the home of the Imperial War Museum. Yet at the turn of the 19th century he had an international reputation as the talented depictor of felines and their foibles in countless magazines, annuals and posters. His paintings and cartoons are now prized by collectors. Beyond his studio he was a notable figure in the National Cat Club and supported many cats' homes and shelters for strays.

By the 1920s he began to taste the same desolation and mental torture which he had sought to alleviate in felines. Public tastes had changed during the First War and his work was less in demand; since his previous creations had been sold outright there was little in the way of royalties.

He made some money from cinema cartoons but gradually he found himself penniless. The privation and bewilderment proved too much and he was admitted to a public asylum, the lowest of the low, a charge on the State, aged 63. In the following two years word began to spread among his many admirers in the cat and art spheres, until Mrs. Cecil Chesterton made an appeal on his behalf in a magazine. The response was immediate and heart-felt; funds flowed in from many of those who had grown up with his charming cat images. He was moved to Bethlehem, which at that time was intended as a relatively civilised retreat for middle-class mental patients. Though doctors thought he may be able in time to return to a normal life he died in the institution. To the end he remained unassuming and humorous, and was able at times to continue with his drawings.

Louis Wain, the London cat artist sketching in his studio at Kilburn. A prolific worker his market was severely affected by the advent of World War II.

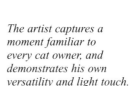

The artist captures a moment familiar to every cat owner, and demonstrates his own versatility and light touch.

Confessions of a Cat-sitter

My career as a London cat-minder was all too brief and ignominious, and you could say it brought tragedy in its train. But I do not blame our feline friends: they have their imperatives as we, poor humans, have our own. So it is best to be chary of excessive sentiment, of being overcome by too-tender feeling – otherwise you too could find yourself one day in a fix exactly like mine . . .

The One That Got Away

STRICTLY, the two cats were not Londoners since they had been brought from Devon as kittens. Both retained, I thought, something of the West Country, a hint of the estuaries and breezy uplands. They quickly learned the London tricks, however, which was as well since they were installed in one of a line of war-time prefabs in Lambeth, within sight of Big Ben.

The mistress worked in the City while the equally youngish master was involved in local government. I first cast eyes on the cats when the couple invited me to their home before their holiday in order to judge whether there was chemistry between myself and the dearly beloveds.

The male cat, Wilfred, clearly dominated the household as of right. His shrewd eyes missed nothing and the shining black coat demanded instant homage. Rosalinda was one of the prettiest felines I have seen, a mottled brown sweetheart, or so it seemed, who loved to leap from the flat roof of the house to the adjoining property for the enjoyment of visitors.

Once or twice the mistress scolded Wilfred for tormenting his companion. "You know Roz doesn't like that," she told him. "She mightn't," the black eyes said, "but I do."

The quadrapeds and I got along well during our two weeks together. There was the occasional attempt to freeze me out – long inexplicable sulks when they took to sleeping on tops of wardrobes and in kitchen cupboards – but I was able to do some writing in the spare room and Wilfred could leave his wet footprints upon the open pages. Rosalinda, it is true, tended to wander off for days, then would re-appear looking pleased and beautiful. Always Wilfred would sidle menacingly toward her, but with intense curiosity, too. "I know where you've been and I think you are *disgusting!*" Roz shrugged off the accusation and slept solidly for three days.

The house had a good-sized garden at the rear and both cats enjoyed playing with tennis balls on the grass or just lying under the shrubs. Then, unexpectedly, they would fling themselves triumphantly through the flap into the kitchen, as if to say, "Feed me." Neither could know that their pleasant life at this address was soon to be brought to a violent end.

Some weeks later another spell of cat-sitting was arranged with the couple and in a contented frame of mind I approached the front door. After a delay, the mistress opened up. "You'd better come in," she said. I noticed a crack in the glass of the door. The pets were not in their usual place before the gas fire in the lounge but were huddled together on a bed in the next room, all rivalry forgotten. "Deadbeats from Waterloo broke in," said the master. "They're watching the place to see when we go out." The couple had cancelled their flight and were moving to the master's small flat in Brixton. Wilf and Roz clung more tightly, eyes averted, pensive for the future.

The new premises were at the top of a five-storey block and the change in the pets' lives was immense; where they had been free spirits, now they were trapped and subdued. The area was too rough to allow them out, the man of the house had declared.

When I acted as their guardian here for the first time I found them brought to the point where their greatest, indeed only, excitement lay in their nightly feeding. Just food junkies, now. Wilfred had discovered a fear of heights and dared not venture near the edge of the balcony. Occasionally he would jump onto the bathroom window sill from the outside and drop down into the tub, but it was a shadow of his daring-do of old. Only in the middle of the night, when the city was still and I lay on a mattress on the living room floor, did they find something of their feline nature. I would waken, and in a drowsy state, become aware of two stealthy creatures leaping like acrobats across my prone body in a secret, macabre game.

As I set out for my second, and fateful, stint at Brixton, I half-vowed to try an experiment. I would open the front door and let the prisoners taste the real world for a brief, revitalising time. Together we would stroll in the sunshine again. So on the third day, one full of the scents of spring, as Rosalinda lurked near the entrance, I took the great decision – the most momentous in her little life – I eased open the door. Roz sniffed the air and her eyes roamed left and right and opened wide to the possibilities. In her manner there appeared an uncharacteristic note of calculation, if only I had noticed.

She stepped hesitantly over the threshold, then with a rush of blood hared off down the stairs, her little feet working with frantic precision. I turned to get the key, then followed her down the stairs, but she was nowhere to be seen. I hurried on, floor after floor, with increasing anxiety. The lobby was empty. She had flown.

Stepping outside I saw at the far end of the building the familiar auburn coat, mixing with other cats. How had they gathered so quickly? Roz, on seeing me, started back, her fangs bared, a terrible hissing sound coming from that well-bred mouth. She was a creature of the wild now, like her new friends. I moved forward and Roz and the other cats turned and raced across the yard, through the car park and over the far fence. I hadn't a chance.

In the flat a bemused Wilfred arranged himself in a corner. Had she really got away? He moved toward the door, interested, then thought better of it. The old brother and sister days were gone.

* * *

Soul-mates in Maida Vale

SURPRISINGLY, after my initial outing as a sitter, I managed one more engagement, but it, too, was to bring humiliation. The household pet did survive my stay – which is more than I can say for the lady's dishwasher.

Again the couple were involved in City business and occupied a terrace house in Maida Vale with all imaginable conveniences. They were a stolid, sober pair, as was their cat, Roger. He had arrived at their door one day in a desolate state, the victim of some unknown trauma. Perhaps he was an abandoned one, unwanted because of a lack of youthful play. Possibly he had known persistent mistreatment.

In his new home he sat all day on the living room floor, non-commital, self-absorbed. He was barred from resting on the sofa – the mistress would not have it – a decision he accepted with equanimity.

I had been hired over the Easter break, and Roger and I soon sank into an agreed pattern. I opened the tins of pet food and cleaned out the litter tray on shedule; he sat in his usual spot all day and all night long – and that was that. It was an adult understanding, and I think in time we came to enjoy each other's presence. There was the odd telephone call from the master of the house checking if everything was alright – checking if I was there at all – but these did not count, and certainly Roger showed not the slightest interest in this intrusion into out solitude.

If I had a complaint it was Roger's refusal to lie on the bed, at my feet, as I slept. I even lifted his large-boned, musty brown body onto the eiderdown in exasperation, but without complaint he merely slipped over the side and returned to his regular place in the front room.

A couple of nights before the owners' return I ventured to try out the lady's smart dishwasher and carefully stacked in the tally of pots and plates that had built up over two or three days, shut the lid, selected the setting and went to view television with Roger.

After some 45 minutes I sensed that he was displaying some unaccustomed interest in the world about him. He seemed almost to be sniffing the air. Very odd. Sniff . . . sniff – my heaven – the dishwasher! I looked sharply at Roger. There was the faintest, most discreet amusement in those distant eyes.

The scene in the kitchen was not promising. The machine appeared to have melted; there was a sickening, pungent smell; a blue mist filled the room. Actually, the rubber padding around the lid and elsewhere had turned to a loose sort of jelly;

some of the plastic, too. A write-off. Surely, I cried, the thing is automatic? Don't they shut themselves off? I felt footpads behind me. Now Roger was at my side. "Nope," he seemed to say.

When Roger saw me packing late the following night he watched with less than his usual inattention. Clearly something was up. Then as I tidied his litter tray and filled up his food bowls for the final time he slowly approached, observed for a while, and all of a sudden began to lick my fingers with a long, dry tongue, as if to say, "We've got along alright – don't you leave me, too." The house was still. It was a touching moment.

Next morning I left the door to the outside hall open, then turned away briefly. When I looked back Roger was almost at the exit and I quickly shut the escape hatch. He had shown unexpected speed.

On my departure he was sitting under the living room window just as he had when I arrived. There was a queer, lonely look about him. I opened the door and with my bag approached the threshold. He looked across at me, and I at him. What an Easter we had spent together. I knew there would never be another.

Newsworthy Cats

Whenever a feline performs some extraordinary act – which, of course, is often – news editors send out their smartest writers knowing that here is certain Page Three material.

Not the notorious Page Threes of the quite awful *Sun*, but the gentler tabloid space of the London *Evening Standard*. In the last years of the 20th century two London cats got the full colour coverage in that journal for exploits that would have warmed the hearts of most commuters as they headed home to their own little pussy . . .

BURIED PUSS. During the Blitz, as the bombs poured down, cats shared the hazards of it all as much as humans. In London many thousands of people died; the feline toll will never be known. Apart from the danger of being under a direct hit a major peril arose from collapsing buildings.

In more recent times, a tabby by name of Fred, showed how prone a cat can be to this risk. In the end luck swung Fred's way, but only after he had spent five days under a pile of debris, clawing and miaowing his head off. When a terrorist bomb exploded at Canary Wharf, in Docklands, in February 1996 whole sides of buildings crashed to the ground, and amid the chaos East Enders wondered whether 1940 had come again.

Fred received only minor cuts from the blast but his path to safety was blocked.

Fred the cat found alive at South Quay 5 days after blast

by PATRICK McGOWAN

A CAT has been found alive by a workman boarding up shattered windows at South Quay five days after the IRA bomb went off.

The workman heard mewing and found the tabby trapped in the rubble of a wrecked building.

The cat, who has been named Fred, was today being cared for by the Cat Protection League, who say he has been deeply traumatised by his ordeal. He crouches in the corner of his cage, shaking in terror if anyone comes near him.

"Poor old thing, he hasn't had a good night at all," said Doreen Ryman who is looking after Fred at her West London home today.

"He is just terribly, terribly frightened and he has only eaten a little. When he was brought in I felt so sorry for him. He was absolutely filthy and very hungry.

"He seems very wild, but that might just be because of th[...] escaped serious injury only to be trapped in the rubble

He had air to breathe but that was all. Days later he heard the faint sound of banging in the distance. It drew nearer and he set up all the miaows he could muster. Workmen were boarding up the broken windows, and though Fred's cries were faint enough through the rubble their feline nature was unmistakeable. The men carefully lifted the broken slabs of concrete, and there dust-covered, wide-eyed and totally relieved was the captive cat.

He was dusted down, checked for major injury, then put in the care of the Cat Protection League. One of its members volunteered to take charge of his rehabilitation in her own home. Was he a wild cat, one of the ferals which wander the vast area of disused wharves and warehouses, a descendant perhaps of the many cats which of old guarded the bulging foodstores against vermin?

After a good wash and some victuals and a brisk brush of his coat Fred seemed more a good-looking pet which had strolled just a little too far from home, while a bomb ticked nearer its appointed time.

JENNY OF HMS BELFAST. Well placed on any list of London tourist venues is this World War II vessel, a veteran of the Battle of North Cape, which now rides at anchor opposite the Tower of London.

It rightly maintains a quiet, satisfied pride, and the tranquil setting matches the ship's mood. Or at least it did – until a three-year-old fox dared venture up the gangplank and onto the vessel during one winter's day in 1997.

Unluckily for the fox there lurked upon the quarter-deck – on guard duty – one

London cat, Midshipman Jennie, who may have been fat for her age, but certainly knew where her resposibility lay. With nose twitching she had immediately sensed the presence of the enemy – now she braced herself for action.

The fox darted into a doorway, but Jennie was after him; truly she was one of Nelson's breed. She caught the foe in the wardroom and it was there that the first battle broke out, with gnashing of teeth, lunging fangs and flying fur. Jenny knew no fear but relentlessly harried the bounder. The sounds of battle alerted crew members, who tried to pull the pair apart.

Each time they dragged Jenny into another room she fought free and hurtled back to the fight. At last she was locked away and the fox captured near a generator, with the help of a baize cloth and a cat box. As the RSPCA took him away to be released the men of HMS Belfast reflected on the firepower, range and unsinkability of their black and white mascot. Pound for pound she ranked with the mightiest guns of the battle fleet.

TOMBSTONE VIGIL

London's most famous cemetery, Highgate, has the power to attract endless visitors each year, with its lineup of elaborate tombs and doleful atmosphere. These qualities even prompted a melancholy Tomcat to adopt one of the tombs as his full-time residence.

The ginger took a particular fancy to the grave of the 19th Century philosopher Herbert Spencer. From his perch on the summit of the tomb he would gaze hour on hour across the path at the nearby resting place of Karl Marx, who had lived much of his later life in London.

It may have been the flow of tourists to the Marx grave which interested him – or was he bringing the old feline magic to bear upon the reign of communism? Within months of his attentions the Red Empire was no more.

ALL HAIL TO THE FELIS LONDINIUM

What makes the cats of London so different? Why do they merit attention? Firstly, there is appearance: the city's street Tom, characteristically, is of stocky build and worldly gaze, and often comes decked in a warming coat of black and white.

Again, how many cats control territory worth a billion pounds or more in real estate terms? On the patch of a City cat an avalanche of shares can change hands each day – not that he cares. He might even lay claim to part of Bond Street or the surrounds of Buckingham Palace. If he scents it – that's his.

• This unique celebration of the capital's felines traces his and her Roman connections, suggested by paw marks set in roof tiles on display at the Museum of London.

• There is Caspar at the Savoy Hotel, an effigy which helps ward off ill fortune; there are the Whittington relics, including a monument to his cat; and at the Army Museum, the redoubtable Crimea Tom.

• Even the aisles of Westminster Abbey have known an assortment of cats over the years, for example Biggles, who particularly enjoyed the choral music. At St. Paul's a black and white Tom operated from a base in the Dean's House; nothing escaped its notice, not even on top of the dome.

London without its felines? You might just as well eliminate Beefeaters or the Changing of the Guard.